"Ooh, I like that," said Roo. "Ask me another one."

"You know," said Owl, "that kind of funny question and answer is called a riddle. I would imagine we could think up some riddles of our own."

"Let's have a riddle contest," cried Roo, "with prizes and everything!"

Just then the rain stopped. The sun came out and shone on the Hundred-Acre Wood.

"Hoo-hoo-hoo!" cried Tigger. "A riddle contest! What fun! I'm going to go out and think up a great riddle. Ta-ta for now!"

As Tigger bounced into the forest, Owl called after him,
"We'll meet before supper outside my house."
The friends all decided to go their separate ways.
Everyone was eager to work on a riddle of his or her own.

When Pooh went back inside his house he headed to his cupboard and took down a pot of honey.

"A smackerel will help me think," he said to himself. "Think, think, think. What should my riddle be about?"

Rabbit went straight to his garden and began pulling weeds. "Gardening always helps me think," he said. "Now what should my riddle be about?"

Inside his own house Owl stared at the family portraits on the wall.

"Funny," he murmured. "Now that I think of it, it seems that many of my esteemed ancestors were chefs. I wonder what kind of riddle Uncle Wolfgang would have thought up . . . or dear Aunt Betty . . . or Cousin Julia?"

    Meanwhile Piglet was so worried about his riddle
that he paced around his living room—back and forth,
around and around.

    "Oh, dear," he said. "What if I can't think up a riddle.
Oh-dear, oh-dear, oh-dear!"

    He picked up some string and nervously began to
untangle it.

Kanga decided that it wouldn't do to worry about making up a riddle. Instead, she took a chair outside and sat down to look at a picture book. At the same time she was keeping an eye on Roo, who was happily playing in the mud left by the morning's rain.

"I'll think up a great riddle, Mama," said Roo.
"Of course you will, dear," Kanga replied.

Eeyore sat in his house and moped.

"Lightning will strike before I think up a decent riddle," he mumbled. "Hmmm . . . maybe I've got something there. . . ."

All day Tigger bounced through the forest, trying to come up with a clever riddle.

"I'm going to win the riddle contest—just watch me!" he said to anyone who would listen.

Then, finally, as the sun slid closer to the tops of the trees, the friends gathered outside Owl's house. It was time for the great riddle contest to begin.

"Since I'm the host," said Owl, "I'll go last. The rule is: whoever tells a riddle that no one can answer will be the winner. Pooh, you go first."

Pooh stepped up on a crate. "What is empty when I am full?" he asked, rubbing his tummy.

"A honey pot!" the others shouted at once.

"Oh, Pooh, that's an easy one," Piglet said with a giggle.

Next it was Rabbit's turn. "What has eyes but cannot see?" he asked.

"That's easy, too," said Owl.

"Yeah," said Tigger. "A potato has eyes but cannot see."

Disappointed, Rabbit stepped down from the crate.

Piglet was next. Trembling slightly, he asked, "What has a long tail and no wings, yet can soar in the breeze?"

"A kite?" Kanga guessed.

"Yep," gulped Piglet as he hopped down from the crate.

Now it was Kanga's turn. "What wears a jacket and has a spine, but is not a living thing?"

The others whispered among themselves and then Owl spoke for the group. "A book?" he guessed.

Kanga smiled as she stepped down. "My, what a clever bunch we are," she said as Roo took his place on the crate.

"What bakes in the sun," Roo began, "melts in the rain, and can be made over and over again?"

The others looked at Roo's dirt-smudged paws. "A mud pie?" everyone answered.

"Gosh," said a disappointed Roo. "I thought no one would guess it!"

Next Eeyore stood on the crate. "Oh, well," he began. "Here goes. What is invisible when it roars and visible when it strikes?"

For a moment no one answered. Then Pooh cried, "I know! A storm with thunder and lightning!"

"Yes, Pooh," Eeyore said sadly as he made way for Tigger.

"Okay," Tigger said happily. "What can do this—the harder it falls down, the higher it bounces back up again?"

Pooh pointed at Tigger. "You!" he answered.

"Naw," Tigger replied. "I never fall down. I win!"

"Wait!" cried Roo. "It's a *ball*!"

Tigger frowned. "Aw, you're right," he said glumly.

Finally Owl took his place on the crate. "All right," he began. "No one has won a prize so far. Now if one of you can guess *my* riddle, you'll *all* win a prize. Answer this: what gets washed after it's cleaned?"

Roo hopped up and down. "I know! I know!" he cried. "A plate! Mama always tells me to clean my plate before she washes it."

"That's correct, Roo," said Owl. "And speaking of dishes, if you'll all follow me, I'll show you your prize."

Owl led his friends to an outdoor table set for a fabulous picnic supper.

As he handed out sandwiches—and a pot of honey to Pooh—Owl decided to try one more riddle. "What listens without complaining," he asked, "shares without asking for anything in return, and often knows you better than you know yourself?"

And then he answered his own riddle:
"A friend! Happy feasting, friends!"